Contents

Any words appearing in the text in bold, **like this**, are explained in the Glossary.

Background to a war

The poets in this book have been called the war poets. This is because they were unlucky enough to be caught up in one of the most horrific and costly wars in human history – the First World War (1914–18). The poems and letters they have left behind give us a unique insight into both the times and the individual people writing them. They help us to understand both the momentous events of this war and their effects on individuals.

The poets came from all sorts of backgrounds; most, but not all, were British. They all had different approaches to the war and they all wrote articulately and passionately. Many of the poets were killed during the war, but some survived and went on to have careers beyond the fighting, and to have families. One survived in body, but his mind was so broken that he never really recovered from the brutality and scale of death he witnessed on the fields of northeastern France. The experiences and ultimate fates of these people were the same as those

Queen Victoria's Diamond Jubilee (June 1897) was celebrated throughout the British Empire in fine military style. Here troops from the colonies march side by side in a unity that would soon be called into question.

C   VES

Poets of the
First World War

NEIL CHAMPION

www.heinemann.co.uk/library
Visit our website to find out more information about **Heinemann Library** books.

To order:
☎ Phone 44 (0) 1865 888066
📄 Send a fax to 44 (0) 1865 314091
💻 Visit the Heinemann Bookshop at www.heinemann.co.uk/library to browse our
catalogue and order online.

First published in Great Britain by Heinemann Library, Halley Court, Jordan Hill, Oxford
OX2 8EJ, a division of Reed Educational and Professional Publishing Ltd. Heinemann is a
registered trademark of Reed Educational and Professional Publishing Ltd.

OXFORD MELBOURNE AUCKLAND JOHANNESBURG BLANTYRE
GABORONE IBADAN PORTSMOUTH NH (USA) CHICAGO

© Reed Educational and Professional Publishing Ltd 2002
First published in paperback 2003
The moral right of the proprietor has been asserted.

Designed by Tinstar Design (www.tinstar.co.uk)
Originated by Ambassador Litho Ltd
Printed and bound by South China Printing Company Ltd in Hong Kong

ISBN 0 431 13996 2   (hardback)   ISBN 0 431 14003 0   (paperback)
06 05 04 03 02   07 06 05 04 03
10 9 8 7 6 5 4 3 2 1   10 9 8 7 6 5 4 3 2 1

British Library Cataloguing in Publication Data
Champion, Neil
    Poets of the First World War. – (Creative Lives)
    1. Poets, English – 20th century – Biography – Juvenile literature
    2. World War, 1914-1918 – Poetry – Juvenile literature
    I.Title
    821.9'12'09

Acknowledgements
The Publishers would like to thank the following for permission to reproduce photographs:
AKG London: p18; BBC Archives: p45; Charterhouse School: p43; Corbis: p44; Hulton Getty
Picture Collection: pp4, 6, 9, 29, 30, 50; Illustrated London News Picture Library: p21;
Imperial War Museum Photography: pp8, 22, 23, 25, 38; John Frost Newspapers: p7; Kings
College, Cambridge: p14; McMaster University, Canada: p27; Mary Evans Picture Library:
p12, 52, 54; National Portrait Gallery, London: p24; Oxford University: pp34, 35, 36, 42;
Oxford University: English Faculty Library: pp31, 32, 41; Robert Harding Picture Library: p46;
Rupert Brooke Society: p15; Topham Picturepoint: p17.

Cover photographs reproduced with permission of Hulton Getty Picture Collection and
Oxford University English Faculty Library.

Extract from the poem *Breakfast* (1914) by Wilfrid Gibson reproduced with permission of
    Macmillan Publishers Limited.
Extract from the poem *For the Fallen* (1914) by Laurence Binyon reproduced with
    permission of The Society of Authors as the Literary Representative of the Estate of
    Laurence Binyon.
Extract from the poem *Base Details* © copyright Siegfried Sassoon. Reproduced by kind
    permission of George Sassoon.
Extract from the poem *The Levellers*, from the 2000 edition of *Complete Poems* by Robert
    Graves, reproduced with permission of Carcanet Press Limited.

Our thanks to Chris Hopkins for his assistance in the preparation of this book.

Every effort has been made to contact copyright holders of any material reproduced in
this book. Any omissions will be rectified in subsequent printings if notice is given to
the Publishers.

of millions of other soldiers. But they were poets – great poets, mostly. They have left us with powerful descriptions of their lives and the feelings they experienced under conditions of the greatest stress and horror imaginable. Their works keep alive the raw emotion and experiences of the war that could otherwise be lost.

Edwardian society

Nearly all the poets covered in this book were born in the 1880s or 1890s. They grew up in late-Victorian Britain, and in the settled Edwardian period that followed. This was a time when the **British Empire** was at its height and ruled over vast territories around the world. Britain was the wealthiest country on Earth and at its most confident, but change was in the air.

Britain was a society dominated by the class system, with strict, though unwritten, rules about how people behaved. The working class, middle class and upper class all had their place, and the poets represented a broad cross-section of these classes, though most came inevitably from the educated sector of society. This is one of the interesting facts about the war and its effect on those who wrote poetry about it – the war threw together people who would never ordinarily have mixed, because they came from such different backgrounds. It would not be true to say that class barriers were broken down, but they were heavily distorted in the unreal and horrific environment of the **trenches**.

Society at the turn of the 20th century was governed by many traditional values inherited from an age that was passing away. Religion played a role in most people's lives. Men held the positions of power in politics, industry and the workplace. Women did not yet have the right to vote in a British general election (this did not happen until 1918, and only then for women aged 30 or over). They were expected to bring up children and obey their husbands in matters of money and the outside world. Of course, in many instances these circumstances did not apply, but in the eyes of society this was how things were meant to work. However, as we shall see, many traditional and accepted notions of human conduct were to change radically during the awful catastrophe that was unleashed in 1914.

Boys at an English public school around the time that the First World War broke out.

A privileged upbringing?

Many of the poets came from privileged middle- or upper-middle-class backgrounds. They went to famous **public schools** such as Marlborough College, Charterhouse and Eton. From there they went on to one of the colleges at Oxford or Cambridge universities. They were well educated and firmly on course to become members of the **establishment**. Others had more ordinary upbringings and a more modest education. As we shall see, the war brought their poetry together, and sometimes the people themselves.

Influences

Some of the war poets met during the war, and many read each other's work and gave comment. They were aware of the early **patriotic** and romanticized work of Rupert Brooke (see pages 11–16), for instance. Although they were never to meet him in person, poets like Charles Sorley (pages 17–21), Wilfred Owen (pages 31–36) and Siegfried Sassoon (pages 37–42) all had views on Brooke and his work. Later on, many of the poets corresponded with each other between bouts of action, or even met up when on home leave or when recovering from wounds. For example, Wilfred Owen and Siegfried Sassoon met as patients at the Craiglockhart Hospital in Scotland in 1917. So the poets were not necessarily isolated writers, though the degree to which they influenced each other's views of the war varied.

Outbreak of conflict

On 28 June 1914, Archduke Ferdinand, the heir to the **Austro-Hungarian Empire**, was assassinated in Sarajevo, Serbia. His killer was a Serbian nationalist, who was hoping to win independence for his country. The **Balkans** provided the spark that then set the rest of Europe alight. Germany stood on the side of her neighbour, Austria-Hungary, against Serbia and its ally, Russia. Britain and France were allied to Russia. When Germany then invaded Belgium, Britain was drawn into the war.

Both sides fought hard early on in the conflict, expecting victory to be quick. In Britain, nearly everyone believed that Germany would soon be defeated: 'It will all be over by Christmas' was the attitude of the public. The **British Expeditionary Force** played a crucial role in helping the French army to halt the German advance into France. But, by November, both sides were exhausted on this 'Western Front' of the war. The troops dug lines of **trenches** as part of their defences, and the pattern for several years of warfare was set. Both sides were roughly equal in numbers and guns, and the result was a **stalemate**. Neither army could gain the upper hand, though both sides launched major offensives, and so the conflict on the Western Front dragged on for four terrible years. In that time, more than 36,000,000 men from all the armies involved in the fighting were killed or wounded.

The front page of the *Daily Mirror* on 5 August 1914, following Britain's declaration of war against Germany.

In 1914 a tide of enthusiasm swept the country as men volunteered to fight for the British cause. Long queues formed outside recruiting offices like this one in Whitehall, London.

Trench warfare

The typical experience of the frontline British soldier was appalling. **Regiments** took their turn to be posted to the trenches, often only a hundred metres away from the German trenches, surrounded by barbed wire. Officers arranged for **sentries** to do night duty and for patrols to go out in the dark into 'no-man's land', the open spaces between the British and German lines. The men would crawl out on their bellies to throw bombs and take pot-shots at German sentries and to try to bring back men who lay wounded from earlier battles. One of the war poets, Siegfried Sassoon (see page 37), became known as 'Mad Jack', because he took more risks on these raids into no-man's land than most would dare. Enemy snipers were constantly shooting at soldiers and artillery kept up a deafening and almost constant barrage.

Relaxation was a rare thing. Another poet, Robert Graves (see pages 43–46), wrote that during one particularly bad period at the frontline, he got about one hour's sleep every night for ten nights in a row. Exhaustion, fear and stress mounted as the weeks at the front went by.

Trenches were often full of water, and were cold in the winter and hot in the summer. As the war dragged on, the landscape became a wasteland, devastated by bombs and filled with craters. The woods and farms of these regions of northern France were obliterated. The fields became littered with the corpses of soldiers.

Early optimism about the war being over by Christmas 1914 soon faded as men got bogged down in the trenches of the Western Front.

Rest and recuperation

The men were relieved by other regiments after each stint at the frontline. They were allowed to move back to towns and villages where they could wash their bodies and clothes, get rid of lice, eat better food and sleep. There they could write their letters home or compose poems in relative peace. But the sound of guns was always present – the big barrages could be heard even back home in England. Many of the soldiers found some sort of consolation in composing verse, as letters home have shown. This did not make them poets, but it does indicate how popular a distraction verse-making could be.

Living conditions were different to anything that the soldiers had ever experienced before. Most soldiers lost the ability to relate to life outside their regiment and the trenches. A large rift developed, often written about by the poets, between the **patriotic** language of glorious heroes and their sacrifice (the view of many politicians and **propagandists**) and the real situation in the fighting lines. Many British soldiers came to have a higher regard for the German soldiers than they did for those whom they felt were profiting from the war and for the bystanders who cheered them off at the ports. These bitter feelings often found their way into the verse of the war poets, especially the poems of Siegfried Sassoon. These were complex emotions that the truly great poets attempted to come to terms with, or at least tried to lay bare for other people to understand.

Major offensives

Occasionally, big offensives (sometimes called 'shows' by the British) were mounted by both sides. Thousands of artillery guns would fire all day and night to flatten the enemy defences. Then the soldiers would go over the top of the trenches to walk across no-man's land, most often into the fire of enemy guns that had not been silenced by the earlier bombardment. The Battle of the Somme is one of the best-known of these offensives. It started in July 1916 and went on until November, but neither side gained much ground. The British suffered 57,000 casualties on the first day alone.

Rupert Brooke

Rupert Chawner Brooke is one of the best-known of the First World War poets. His life and his writing represented the **Romantic**, idealistic and **patriotic** views of the early war years. Brooke was a poet who actually saw very little action – he died early on without having been involved in any of the fighting. However, he has gone down in history as the **epitome** of the noble young man making the ultimate sacrifice for his country – that of laying down his life.

The young Brooke

Rupert Brooke was born on 3 August 1887, at 5 Hillmorton Road in the town of Rugby in Warwickshire. He came from the upper-middle class and his short life reflects the concerns of, and changes in, this section of society during this period.

Rupert Brooke's father was a **housemaster** at Rugby School, one of England's most famous **public schools**. Brooke had two brothers, one older and one younger than himself. He was educated first of all at a private school in Rugby and then at a **preparatory school**, Hillbrow. He left there in 1901 at the age of fourteen to go to the school in Rugby where his father taught.

At Rugby Public School, Brooke received the best education the country had to give. While at the school, he became a member of the **cadet corps**. This does not necessarily indicate that he wanted to join the army, as most boys from a similar background at public school joined the cadet corps – it was part of school life. Indeed, it was here that Brooke first started to experiment with writing poetry, mainly in a style that imitated the Romantic poets.

Cambridge and beyond

Rupert Brooke left school and went to Kings College, Cambridge. He was a bright student and good at games such as cricket. At Cambridge he joined the Fabians (see box on page 13), a society set up in 1884 by **socialist** thinkers. At this society Brooke met with some of the most famous Fabians of his day, including the Irish playwright George Bernard Shaw (1856–1950).

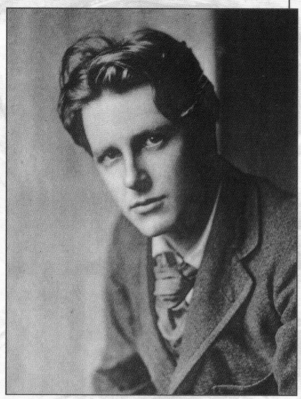

Rupert Brooke, 'the most handsome man in England', posing for a portrait photograph in 1913.

The Irish poet W. B. Yeats called Brooke 'The most handsome man in England', and in verse he was celebrated by a friend (Frances Cornford, the granddaughter of Charles Darwin) as 'Young Apollo, golden-haired'. Throughout his life he attracted great attention, partly because of his good looks, but also through his connections in society. He mixed with many of the influential writers and politicians of the time, including E. M. Forster, Maynard Keynes, Virginia Woolf and Edward Thomas.

Brooke **graduated** in 1909 and went to travel in Germany and Italy. In 1911 his first book of verse, *Poems 1911*, was published. He went travelling again in 1913 and 1914, this time in North America and the Pacific, writing articles for *The Times* newspaper. He fell in love with a Samoan girl called Taatamata and wrote a poem for her, *Tiare Tahiti*.

War as 'adventurous romance'

Brooke had returned to England by the time the war started. Following the popular mood of the time, he immediately joined up. There was a feeling at the outbreak of the war that it would not last too long. The glory and position of England on the world stage were at stake and young men like Brooke eagerly signed up for the fighting. They did not want to be left out.

Rupert Brooke joined the Royal Naval Division in 1914 as a **sub-lieutenant** and took part in a military expedition to Antwerp in

Brooke and the Fabian Society

The Fabian Society was a socialist society founded in England in 1884 by Sidney and Beatrice Webb, who were heavily involved in the development of socialist economic and political policies. The society was named after a Roman general, Fabius Maximus, who died in 203 BCE. In battle, Fabius had used the tactic of stealth (moving carefully and quietly to avoid detection) rather than head-on conflict. The 19th century had been a period of bloody revolution, from the aftermath of the French Revolution and Napoleon's time of power, through the revolutions that swept Europe in 1830 and again in 1848, to the time of deep unrest in Russia in the second half of the century. The Fabians wanted to reform society to favour the poor and underprivileged, but not through revolution or other forms of direct conflict with the state.

Holland. It was at this time that he wrote three of his war sonnets, *Peace, Safety* and *The Soldier*. These were some of the earliest poems about the notion of going off to war as a cleansing and dignified act. The sonnets were published in December 1914 and were instantly used by people to support the British war effort. However, they were attacked by later poets as not being based on any real experience. Brooke's works were most often quoted by the **propagandists** and manipulators, who used his sentiments to fire up passion for the British cause. Even the Dean of St Paul's Cathedral in London was to quote from *The Soldier* in a sermon early in 1915, saying that 'the enthusiasm of a pure and elevated patriotism had never found a nobler expression'.

"
Brooke's poems are amongst the most frequently read from this period, with *The Soldier* being probably the most popular British First World War poem. Its immortal opening lines read:

'If I should die, think only this of me:
That there's some corner of a foreign field
That is forever England...'
"

Off to war

In February 1915 Brooke's unit left for the eastern Mediterranean, heading for the conflict against the Turkish at Gallipoli. He wrote in one of his last letters from on board his ship:

'I've never been quite so happy in my life, I think. Not quite so pervasively happy; like a stream flowing entirely to one end. I suddenly realise that the ambition of my life has been – since I was two – to go on a military expedition against Constantinople.'

He was never to arrive. He contracted blood poisoning from a mosquito bite on board a ship in the Mediterranean and died on 23 April 1915, aged 28. Rupert Brooke did not live to experience the long drawn-out horror of the war.

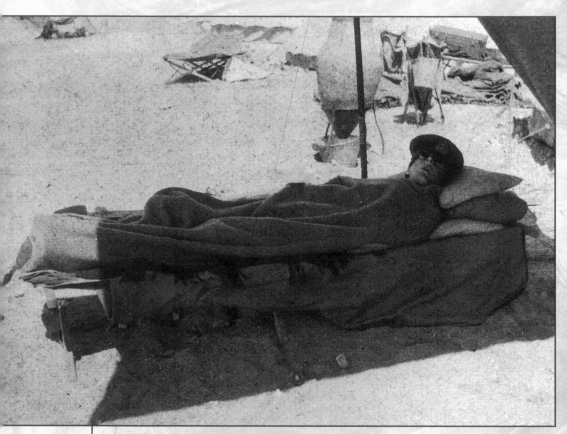

Rupert Brooke laid out on a stretcher in the shade of a tree. Here he died on 23 April 1915 from blood poisoning, his dream of fighting nobly for his country having come to nothing.

The inscription on Rupert Brooke's grave on the Greek island of Skyros reads, 'If I should die, think only this of me: That there's some corner of a foreign field That is for ever England.'

"

'The thoughts to which he gave expression in the very few incomparable war sonnets which he left behind will be shared by many thousands of young men moving resolutely and **blithely** forward into this, the hardest, cruellest, and the least-rewarded of all the wars men have fought. They are a whole history and revelation of Rupert Brooke himself. Joyous, fearless, versatile, deeply instructed, with classic **symmetry** of mind and body, he was all that one would wish England's noblest sons to be in days when no sacrifice but the most precious is acceptable, and the most precious is that which is most freely **proffered**.'

An obituary for Rupert Brooke in The Times newspaper, 26 April 1915, written by Winston Churchill, then First Lord of the Admiralty

> "
> 'Blow out, you bugles, over the rich Dead!
> There's none of these so lonely and poor of old,
> But, dying, has made us rarer gifts than gold.
> These laid the world away; poured out the red
> Sweet wine of youth; gave up the years to be
> Of work and joy, and that unhoped serene,
> That men call age; and those who would have been,
> Their sons, they gave, their immortality.'
> From Brooke's poem *The Dead*, 1914
> "

However, the few sonnets Brooke wrote about the war have given him a place of honour in the hearts and minds of the nation. There is a memorial to him on the Greek island of Skyros where he is buried. There is also one at his school, Rugby, containing a sculpture of him and the words from his poem *The Soldier*.

After his death, Brooke's work and example were used by the **establishment** of the day to bolster the war effort. Britain needed enthusiastic young men to go to the front, especially those from backgrounds (mainly middle- and upper-class) that enabled them to enter the ranks as officers. Brooke's 'willing sacrifice', laying down his life for the cause of the war effort, was reported time and again. It was designed to inspire and goad others to make the same sacrifice. Brooke's poems largely support this view. But then, Brooke did not live long enough to see the war drag on and literally millions die on the battlefields of France. We cannot know how his view might have changed. Many of his fellow poet soldiers came to reject totally his upbeat and patriotic interpretation of events, as we shall see.

Gallipoli

On 1 November 1914, Turkey entered the war on the side of Germany. Turkey attacked Russia. Winston Churchill sent troops (mainly from Australia and New Zealand) to attack the Turkish port of Gallipoli. The attack was a failure. Around 36,000 British and Commonwealth soldiers died. Rupert Brooke never lived to see the disaster take place. He died en route.

Charles Sorley

Charles Hamilton Sorley was very different in character to Rupert Brooke. He never got caught up in the **patriotic** tide or swept away by enthusiasm for the British cause. He left behind many fine poems and letters that reveal a complex approach to the devastating times in which he found himself living.

Early life

Charles Sorley was born in Aberdeen in Scotland on 19 May 1895. His father was Professor of Moral Philosophy at Aberdeen University. Sorley's upbringing greatly contributed to his individual and intellectual approach to the moral questions surrounding the war. He grew up a very bright child and won a **scholarship** to Marlborough College, a large and renowned **public school** in the south of England. In 1913 he won a further scholarship to go to Oxford University. Before taking up his place, he made the decision to spend some time in Germany, studying German language and literature. He went in January 1914, and by April had attached himself to the University of Jena, where he started studying.

Charles Hamilton Sorley, in a portrait photograph taken just before the outbreak of the First World War. Though he died young, the poems he left behind show a complex and mature approach to the fighting.

Attitudes to the war

Sorley was overtaken by the momentous events of the declaration of war while on a hiking holiday in Germany. Perhaps not surprisingly, being British, he was soon taken into custody

The English public school

Charles Sorley was born in Aberdeen but, like so many of his contemporaries from middle-class backgrounds, he was sent off to board at an English public school. Boarding meant that during the school term, the pupils ate and slept at the school. Everything revolved around school life for these young boys – they lived and breathed it all day, every day, until the end of term came and they were allowed home to see their parents. Sorley went to Marlborough which, along with Eton, Winchester and a handful of other establishments, is one of the country's most prestigious public schools.

and imprisoned. He was, however, quickly released and ordered to leave the country.

Sorley had begun to write poems before the war broke out. Although only a young man, he had formed mature opinions about many issues. During his lengthy stay in Germany, he had come to respect the German people and their traditions. His feelings for his own country were more complicated.

A student drinking quarter in the German town of Jena around the time that Charles Sorley was studying at the university.

Although Sorley was not a **pacifist**, he did not believe in the 'just' British cause against a so-called detested enemy. He put very clearly his dislike of the **populist** patriotic mood sweeping the England that he had returned to in a letter of November 1914: 'England – I am sick of the sound of the word. In training to fight for England, I am training to fight for that deliberate **hypocrisy**, that terrible middle class **sloth** of outlook… that has marked us out from generation to generation.'

In the same letter he went on to say: 'And yet we have the impudence to write down Germany… as "Huns" [an insulting term for Germans].' In acknowledgement of his own position, he said: 'But all these convictions are useless for me to state since I have not the courage for them. What a worm one is under the cart-wheels… of public opinion. I might have been giving my mind to fight against Sloth and Stupidity; instead, I am giving my body… to fight against the most **enterprising** nation in the world.'

This was a brutally honest letter written by a man who had seen through the patriotic speeches of politicians and the newspapers – but who could not bring himself to stand out against public opinion and oppose the war. Many people did, and many were put into prison.

Serving at the front

In 1915 Sorley joined the Suffolk **Regiment**, taking training as an officer and leaving for the front as a lieutenant in May 1915. He was promoted to captain within three months of arriving in France.

Although Sorley was a Christian (he mentioned in a letter that he had strong religious instincts), his poetry does not provide a comfortable vision of life after death. Instead, it focuses on the suffering he saw around him in the frontline of battle.

In 1915, while serving in France, Sorley wrote a war poem called *When You See Millions of the Mouthless Dead*. It has often been interpreted as a poetic response to Brooke's *The Soldier* (see page 13). It does not tell people that all those soldiers who have been killed have died for a just cause. It gives the stark message: 'They are dead.' Sorley was not a man to hide from what he saw as the truth.

"

'When you see millions of the mouthless dead
Across your dreams in pale **battalions** go,
Say not soft things as other men have said,
That you'll remember. For you need not so.
Give them not praise. For, deaf, how should they know
It is not curses heaped on each gashed head?
Nor tears. Their blind eyes see not your tears flow.
Nor honour. It is easy to be dead.
Say only this, "They are dead." Then add thereto,
"yet many a better one has died before."
Then, scanning all the overcrowded mass, should you
Perceive one face that you loved heretofore,
It is a spook. None wears the face you knew.
Great death has made all this for evermore.'
Sorley's poem *When You See Millions of the Mouthless Dead*, 1915

"

However, there are signs that Sorley eventually came to accept the fighting and the fact of being there. In August 1915 he wrote:

'… out in front at night in that no-man's land and long graveyard there is a freedom and a spur. Rustling of the grasses and grave tap-tapping of distant workers: the tension and silence of encounter, when one struggles in the dark for moral victory over the enemy patrol: the wail of the exploded bomb and the animal cries of wounded men. Then death and the horrible thankfulness when one sees that the next man is dead… One is hardened now: **purged** of all false pity…'

Like Brooke, Sorley died early in the war. But his attitude to the events that overtook him was vastly different. Brooke died a little before him, and in a letter of Sorley's we hear his characteristic frankness as he talks about a fellow soldier and poet's death:

'I saw Rupert Brooke's death in *The Morning Post*… I think Brooke's early poems – especially notably *The Fish* and *Grantchester*… are his best. That last sonnet-sequence of his which has been so praised I find… overpraised. He is far too obsessed with his own sacrifice, regarding the going to war of himself... as a highly intense, remarkable and sacrificial exploit, whereas it is merely the conduct demanded of him (and others) by the turn of the circumstance... He has clothed his attitude in fine words: but he has taken the **sentimental** attitude.'

Charles Sorley was killed on 13 October 1915 by a German sniper at the Battle of Loos in northeastern France. He was still only twenty years old. The year after, *Marlborough and Other Poems* was published. This collection of his verse was popular at the time, though not nearly as popular as the poems of the men who wrote patriotic and stirring pieces for the masses.

The terrible aftermath of the Battle of Loos in 1915. It was during this 'show' that Sorley was killed, at the age of just twenty.

Isaac Rosenberg

Isaac Rosenberg had a unique vision of the world, which came from his position as an outsider. He came from a poor, working-class Jewish family. He did not go to a **public school** or university. He did not fight in the war as an officer, but as an ordinary **private soldier**. And so his perspective on society and the war was different to many of the other poets featured in this book.

The East End of London

Isaac Rosenberg was born in Bristol on 25 November 1890, the son of Jewish immigrants from Russia. They had left that country because of what we would today call **religious persecution** under the

government of the Russian Tsar (king). In 1897 the family moved to the East End of London, where there was the promise of better living standards and opportunities for work for Rosenberg's father. Isaac Rosenberg's health suffered in London, however. His lungs were weakened by city life and he grew into a frail and small adult.

Rosenberg went to school locally in Stepney. At the age of fourteen he left school and became an apprentice engraver. It was not the kind of work that he wanted to do. He said in a letter that 'It is horrible to think that all these hours, when my days are full of

Isaac Rosenberg in military uniform. This photographic portrait was taken of the young poet shortly before he went to France to join his regiment, called the Bantams.

Cable Street in the East End of London. Six-year-old Isaac Rosenberg and his family moved here in 1897. He was to grow up in a tight-knit Jewish community in the area.

vigour and my hands craving for self-expression, I am bound, chained... without hope and almost desire of deliverance...'

Art school

However, deliverance *was* at hand. Rosenberg was aware of his creative talent from an early age and knew that his apprenticeship gave him no opportunity to express it. So he first looked to painting, attending evening classes at the art school at Birkbeck College. There his talent was recognized by three Jewish women who were willing and able to become his **patrons** – the Jewish community in the East End was tight-knit, and many did what they could to support the less fortunate amongst them. The women paid for him to study at the Slade School of Fine Art.

But Rosenberg had another pull on his creative talents – that of poetry. He wrote of the dilemma he found himself in: 'I really would like to take painting seriously; I think I might do something at that; but poetry – I despair of ever writing excellent poetry. I can't look at things in the simple, large way that great poets do.'

23

Isaac Rosenberg's first artistic passion was for painting. This is a self-portrait, done in 1915.

South Africa

In the early summer of 1914 Rosenberg made the decision to travel to Cape Town in South Africa, where one of his sisters was living. He wanted to do something for his frail health, and moving to a country with a better climate seemed a good idea. He was by this time 23 years old. He was poor but in good spirits, writing home to say that 'I am living like a toff here'.

However, the adventure was not to last. War broke out in Europe in August of the same year, and Rosenberg returned in 1915 to try to enlist in the army. His reasons for joining are not obvious. He was not a **patriot** and he did not identify with the British, who mainly felt enthusiastic about the war. He felt something of an outsider. His family did not want him to fight in the war either. He says in one letter written during this period: 'I have changed my mind again about joining the army. I feel about it that more men means more war, – besides the immorality of joining with no patriotic convictions.'

However, Rosenberg eventually joined the army, in October 1915. Other letters give us a few clues as to why: 'I never joined the army for patriotic reasons. Nothing can justify war. I suppose we all must fight to get the trouble over.' And in another: 'There is certainly a strong temptation to join when you are making no money.'

'I am determined that this war, with all its powers for devastation, shall not master my poeting… I will not leave a corner of my consciousness covered up, but saturate myself with the strange and extraordinary new conditions of this life, and it will all refine itself into poetry later on.'

From a letter Rosenberg wrote in 1916

In the army

Rosenberg had initially been refused entry into the regular army because of his very small size. However, he joined a specially formed **regiment** called the Bantams. This catered for men too short to be accepted into other regiments. He was sent to France and lived and fought for two years in the terrible conditions of the Western Front. As in ordinary society, he found himself the outsider – his Jewishness and no doubt his size made him an easy target for abuse by soldiers already brutalized by war in the **trenches**. However, he came to the front with his poetic life in full bloom. 'I believe in myself more as a poet than a painter. I think I get more depth into my writing,' he wrote in a letter from the front.

Just before going to France, Rosenberg had published a volume of verse called *Youth*. During his two years in France, he added more poems with war as their theme, including *Break of Day in the Trenches*, *God*, *Louse Hunting* and *Dead Man's Dump*.

A photograph of Rosenberg's regiment, the Bantams, training for combat in Cheshire in 1915.

> " *Dead Man's Dump*, which Rosenberg wrote in 1917, was the longest and most expressive poem he wrote about the war. It opens with these startling and memorable lines: "
>
> *'A man's brains splattered on*
> *A stretcher-bearer's face;*
> *His shook shoulders slipped their load*
> *But when they bent to look again*
> *The dreaming soul was sunk too deep*
> *For human tenderness.'*

Army life

Isaac Rosenberg spent his two years in the army hating much about the type of life he was leading. He was a working-class Jewish poet who was now a private in the British Army. The food was terrible, the hygiene not what he was used to, and the routine of training and petty tasks often very dull. He complained in one letter that his boots had taken all the skin off his feet. Marching had become unbearable, which obviously presented a big problem to an ordinary soldier. He also had to put up with **anti-Semitic** abuse from other soldiers. At one point he requested transfer to a Jewish **battalion** fighting in North Africa, but was not successful.

Life in the trenches in 1917 and 1918 is captured in some detail in Rosenberg's poems – for example, in *In the Trenches*, *Break of Day in the Trenches* and *Returning, We Hear Larks*. He tells of the usual mixture of being at the frontline, living in constant fear of sudden death from a sniper's bullet or an unlucky bomb, and resting behind the lines, trying to catch up on laundry, eating, washing the body and writing letters and poems. He was resting behind the lines in spring 1918 when orders came through to move up to the front.

Isaac Rosenberg was killed on 1 April 1918. His body was never recovered so it is not known how he died. He left behind poems of power and great compassion, written both before and during the war. He was not to find much of an audience for his works during or even shortly after his life, but later critics have seen them as evidence of a great mind and talent that was cruelly cut down in the last year of the 'Great War'.

Vera Brittain

Vera Brittain is different from many of the poets in this selection. As a woman, she was not allowed to serve as a combatant, but she volunteered instead for the female equivalent – serving at the front as a **Voluntary Aid Detachment** (VAD) nurse. There she saw sights as horrific as any of those seen by the soldiers she was caring for. Vera Brittain wrote one of the most famous pieces of autobiography dealing with this period of history – *Testament of Youth*. She was also personally touched by the war's tragic slaughter, as her brother, Edward, and fiancé, Roland Leighton, were both killed in the fighting.

A struggle for education

Vera Mary Brittain was born in Newcastle-under-Lyme in 1893. Her father, Thomas Brittain, was a wealthy paper manufacturer. Vera was educated at home by a **governess** and then sent to a girl's boarding school in Surrey. She was being educated for the life of an ordinary middle-class woman in early 20th-century England – groomed to become a wife and mother. However, she had strong views about what she wanted, and was determined to go to Oxford University to study English Literature. Her father finally relented, and in October 1914 she went to Somerville College, a women's college at Oxford. She said that 'When the Great War broke out, it came to me not as a **superlative** tragedy, but as an interruption of the most exasperating kind to my personal plans.'

A young Vera Brittain (front row, centre) poses for a family photograph in the years before the war.

Despite having to give up the university place for which she had struggled so hard, Vera Brittain wanted to help with the war effort, and she became one of the first women at the college to do so. She became a VAD

27

nurse in 1915. But tragedy was to follow. In 1914 she had met and later become engaged to Roland Leighton, a school friend of her only brother, Edward. In December 1915, Leighton was killed by a German sniper whilst fighting in France.

However, Vera Brittain kept to her aim of becoming a writer, in spite of the war. She turned to poetry at this time of emotion and intensity, and also wrote letters home and kept a personal diary.

At the frontline

As a nurse, Vera Brittain was initially sent to Malta, in 1916, and then served on the Western Front from August 1917. She witnessed first-hand the horrific wounds soldiers suffered during the war, and was eventually to become a life-long **pacifist** as a result of these experiences. She played a part in looking after the hundreds of thousands of casualties from the Passchendaele offensive in that year. This included caring for wounded German prisoners of war, an experience she found strange, and which she wrote about in both her poetry and in *Testament of Youth*:

'Before the War I had never been in Germany and had hardly met any Germans... So it was somewhat disconcerting to be... in the midst of thirty representatives of the nation which, as I had repeatedly been told, had crucified Canadians, cut off the hands of babies and subjected... females to unmentionable "atrocities". I didn't think I had believed all those stories, but I wasn't quite sure.'

She wrote poems throughout the war period, which were collected and published in 1919 under the title, *Verses of a VAD*. This volume contains the poems *To My Brother*, *Perhaps* and *The German Ward*. In *Perhaps*, she remembers her fiancé, Roland. *To My Brother* describes the wounds her brother had received in the Battle of the Somme:

'Your battle-wounds are scars upon my heart,
Received when in that grand and tragic 'show'
You played your part...'

Although he survived the Somme, Edward was killed in 1918 while fighting on the Italian front.

A changed world

After the war, Vera Brittain finally **graduated** from university in 1921, having studied History, and then moved to London. She became a writer and a journalist. She had become more left-wing in her politics and joined the Labour Party around this time. She even considered standing for Parliament. However, she married an American called George Catlin and for a while lived in the USA. Her second child, Shirley, was born in 1930. Baroness Shirley Williams, as she is known today, is still a prominent member of the British political world.

Vera Brittain joined the Voluntary Aid Detachment (VAD) as a nurse in 1915, when she was 22 years old.

Vera Brittain, like many others, was appalled by the atrocities of the First World War. But the war brought her and many other women greater liberation. Under normal circumstances as a young middle-class woman, she would have owed her time first of all to her parents, and then – once married – to her husband and their children. The war changed all that for her and for a whole generation of women. Working in factories at home, or serving abroad as Brittain had done, had given women a new taste of freedom. They had found that they could be independent, and many were inspired to fight for equal rights with men.

29

'Didn't women experience the war as well?'

This was the question that drove Vera Brittain to write some of the most moving and popular accounts of those terrible years. *Testament of Youth* was published in 1933, and it gives a woman's view – her view – of the tragic times she had lived through. It adds to the personal accounts of the war given by Siegfried Sassoon (see pages 37–42), Robert Graves (pages 43–46), and others. In her account, Brittain says that her aim is 'to tell history in terms of personal life'.

Through her autobiographical writing, poems and journalism, Vera Brittain worked to move the cause of women's rights forward. She also found expression for her deep conviction about pacifism, the non-violent and democratic resolution of problems between nations without recourse to weapons and bloodshed. In 1957 she helped to found the Campaign for Nuclear Disarmament (CND). Vera Brittain died in 1970, having written to a friend not long before that 'I shall welcome death when it comes because it will release me from remembering the things I still have to remember.' At her request her ashes were scattered over her brother's grave in Italy.

Vera Brittain (second from right) demonstrating outside Lancaster House in London in 1961, against the Sharpeville Massacre in South Africa in which 69 blacks were killed by police. Brittain remained a passionate advocate of freedom and democracy throughout her life.

Wilfred Owen

Wilfred Owen was probably the greatest of the poets writing about the First World War. He is also one of the best known. His poems, such as *Strange Meeting*, *Dulce Et Decorum Est*, *Futility* and *At a Calvary near the Ancre*, are still read as profound statements on war and its degrading effects on human relationships.

Oswestry and beyond

Wilfred Edward Salter Owen was born on 18 March 1893 at the family home of Plas Wilmot in Oswestry, a town on the border between England and Wales. Tom Owen, his father, worked on the railways. His mother, Susan, was a strong-willed woman who harboured ambitious thoughts for her son's future. The family suffered financial problems in 1897 when Wilfred's grandfather died in debt. They were forced to move from the large family house.

Tom Owen got work at Birkenhead near Liverpool as stationmaster, and the family moved to 14 Willmer Road. Wilfred went to school at the Birkenhead Institute and showed early signs of being bookish.

A photograph taken of three generations of the Owen family in 1895 outside their home, Plas Wilmot, on the Welsh border. Two-year-old Wilfred is sitting on his mother's knee.

He also showed an interest in poetry. As his brother Harold recounted much later:

'It was… among the ferns and bracken and the little hills, secure in the safety and understanding love that my mother wrapped about him with such tender ministration, that the poetry in Wilfred, with gentle pushings, without hurt, began to bud, and not on the battlefields of France.'

The family had financial struggles, but they clung to middle-class ideas about the importance of education and culture. Wilfred had piano lessons. His mother was very religious and opposed to alcohol, and Wilfred was made to become a member of a **temperance society**. This **puritan** streak stayed with him all his life. School life and family holidays in Ireland, Cornwall and their beloved Wales complete a picture of a happy childhood and strong family bonds.

Owen in France with the poet, Laurent Tailhade, shortly before the outbreak of the First World War.

Discovering poetry

In 1906, Wilfred's father got a promotion and early the following year the family moved to Shrewsbury, where his new job was located. Wilfred went to the Shrewsbury **Technical School**, where he excelled in French. He also read some of the great works of English literature, including many Shakespeare plays and the **Romantic** poetry of Keats and Shelley, all of which influenced his later writing. He became attached to religious study as well, no doubt influenced by his mother.

After leaving the school, Owen worked for a while as an assistant teacher. He failed to get high enough marks in his **matriculation** exams for the University of London to gain a **scholarship**. Instead he went to work in late 1911 as an assistant to the Reverend Herbert Wigan at Dunsden Vicarage in Oxfordshire. Owen was writing poetry at this time – he even won second prize in a Bible Society competition. He witnessed a funeral at Dunsden, which inspired him to write his best poems of that period.

Owen was happy in his new post at Dunsden, but suffered from poor health. He had weak lungs, and after a spell in bed with bronchitis, his doctor advised him to take time out in the south of France, where the climate would help his condition. So, in September 1913, he left for the city of Bordeaux, where he had arranged to teach part-time at the Berlitz Language School.

War breaks out

Owen was still in France when war with Germany broke out in August 1914. He did not rush to join the army. In fact, he wrote about his own feeling of being isolated from the action:

'I went to visit the battlefield of Castillon, where, in 1453 Talbot Earl of Shrewsbury suffered defeat… I can't understand it, but this battlefield will interest me as much as the field of Marne… [where French soldiers had famously defeated a German offensive earlier in 1914].'

However, after a visit to the hospital in Bordeaux and witnessing the wounds of soldiers, Owen's conscience was touched. He returned to England in the late summer of 1915 and had joined the army by October. Although he had mixed feelings about the fighting, ultimately his sense of the suffering of others brought out his deep-seated feelings of pity. Owen felt the need to do something to ease or even stop that suffering. In June 1916 he was commissioned into the Manchester **Regiment** and was sent for training. He found army life hard. He was up at 6.30 a.m. for drill (military exercises) followed by a lecture and training. The day ended with polishing boots and cleaning one's gun and uniform.

A photograph of Wilfred Owen in uniform (front row, second from right), taken in July 1916. He is with fellow soldiers from the Manchester Regiment.

In 1916 Owen was based for a while in Aldershot. He went to Dunsden to see the vicarage. His former employer said brightly to him 'the war will be over very soon', echoing the commonly held **civilian** view. Owen's brother Harold noted that Wilfred initially saw the war as a disruption to his poetry, to both the reading and writing of it.

War and poetry

As we have seen, Owen had already discovered his attraction to poetry before the outbreak of the war. It had come to dominate his life and thoughts. When he was sent to the Western Front he felt a deep compassion for his fellow soldiers that was to grow and strengthen as the war progressed. What Owen was then able to achieve in verse was a union of his poetic genius with his feelings about the situation that he and his men found themselves in. He wrote with outrage about the wilful ignorance of the civilians and politicians back home, who had no idea of the real conditions under which the soldiers lived and died. And he expressed great compassion and pity for the men who suffered. Early on he felt the typical soldier's elation at being at the front. He wrote, 'There is a fine heroic feeling about being in France… but excitement is always necessary to my happiness.' But as the horrors grew in number and the senselessness of the suffering became more apparent, so his anger grew and the poet in him rose up and responded. This is evident in such poems as *Dulce et Decorum Est* (written in October 1917), *Soldier's Dream* (also October 1917) and *Spring Offensive* (September 1918).

Meeting with Sassoon

In 1917 a meeting took place that changed Owen. He was involved in heavy fighting on the front when he was knocked unconscious by a shell that exploded nearby. He spent several days in a bomb crater before being rescued. Owen was sent to recover from **shell shock**

An early draft of one of Wilfred Owen's poems, written in his own handwriting. It is *Dulce et Decorum Est*, written in October 1917.

at a hospital in Scotland called Craiglockhart. Whilst recovering there, he met Siegfried Sassoon, another soldier and poet (see pages 37–42). Sassoon became a friend, mentor and source of inspiration to Owen. After their meeting Owen wrote: 'And you have fixed my life – however short. You did not light me; I was always a mad comet; but you have fixed me…'

By 'fixed' Owen probably meant that Sassoon had given him some purpose or direction, at least to his poetic life. Sassoon encouraged Owen to write more direct poems, using the speech of everyday life. He also encouraged him to express openly the anger and disgust he felt at the callous spending of soldiers' lives by people safe in London.

> "
> Owen's poems show the pity – the waste – of the war. He wrote of his work that 'the poetry is in the pity'. This can be seen in one of his well-known war poems, *Futility*, which opens with the lines:
> "
>
> 'Move him into the sun –
> Gently its touch awakes him once…
> If anything might rouse him now
> The kind old sun will know.'

Only four of Owen's poems were published during his short life. **Posthumous** collections (the first arranged by Siegfried Sassoon in 1920, called *Collected Poems*) and **anthologies** have kept his name alive. Owen also had a younger brother, Harold, who wrote an autobiography called *Journey from Obscurity*. Both Sassoon and Harold Owen have left tributes to Owen.

The death of Wilfred Owen

On leaving Craiglockhart in late October 1917, Owen was given a job instructing new recruits. It was a safe time, in England, away from the fighting. But Owen's conscience would not let him rest easy. He felt uncomfortable being a long way behind the lines when he knew what his men were going through in France. By August 1918 he was back in the **trenches** with his **battalion**. Here he felt that he would 'be better able to cry my outcry, playing my part'. He was fully aware of what he had done, writing to Sassoon about his 'foolish' decision. 'This is what the shells scream at me every time: Haven't you got the wits to keep out of this?'

By now the British Army and its allies had finally broken free of the **stalemate** of the trenches, and were forcing the German Army back. Owen was killed on 4 November, one week before the war finally ended, while trying to cross a canal with his men. His parents received news of his death on the day that church bells rang out all over Britain, heralding a new time of peace.

The Craiglockhart War Hospital in Edinburgh, where Wilfred Owen and Siegfried Sassoon met in 1917 and discussed poetry.

Siegfried Sassoon

Siegfried Sassoon is one of the most important poets who fought in the First World War. His privileged background, Jewish roots and **homosexuality** all contributed to make him a complex and often contradictory personality. Sometimes he could be courageous to the point of foolhardiness (he was nicknamed 'Mad Jack' by his fellow soldiers) and at other times, he could be very introverted and shy – he was both a man of action and a quiet thinker. Not only did he write some of the most memorable and **satirical** poems of the war, condemning the 'Old Men' who sent the young to their deaths, he also managed to survive the conflict and live for nearly 50 years after the **Armistice**.

Childhood in Kent

By his own admission, Sassoon's upbringing was a very happy affair. He was born on 8 September 1886 at a large 'gentleman's' house (it had nine bedrooms) called Weirleigh, near Paddock Wood in Kent. Sassoon retained fond memories of this first home throughout his life. His father, Alfred, added a studio and stables to it. Siegfried's family on his father's side, the Sassoons, were Jewish and very wealthy. His mother's side, the Thornycrofts, were English farmers from Cheshire. According to family tales, the two families were so different in character that they rarely understood each other.

Education

In 1900, Sassoon went to the New Beacon **Preparatory School** near Sevenoaks, about 14 miles from his home. He remained there for about two years and then, like Charles Sorley (see pages 17–21), went to one of the biggest and most famous **public schools** in England, Marlborough College. He boarded at the school during term time, going home only for the holidays. His mother had become very possessive of him, always concerned about his health, and when he left it was something of a wrench.

In 1905 Sassoon went to Clare College at Cambridge University to study Law. However, he did not like his chosen subject and changed it to History. Overall he was not happy at university. He was beginning to write poetry seriously by this time, and much of his energy went in this direction. He did not finish his course, staying for only four terms. He finally left in March 1907, without any idea of what he was going to do with his life.

The country gentleman

For the next seven years, Sassoon lived at home in Kent and in London, leading the life of a country gentleman and man of letters. He filled his time in the country playing golf, cricket, **steeple-chasing** and fox hunting. He even took to smoking a pipe (although only in his early twenties) to finish off the image of a country squire. In London, he bought books, visited art galleries and went to concerts. He also joined a gentleman's club, and did not neglect his tailors and bootmakers. He had thrown himself into the role with all his energy. He was also writing poetry, mainly in a late-**Romantic** style. Between 1908 and 1913, he produced nine volumes of verse.

Outbreak of war

When war in Europe came in August 1914, Sassoon wrote that he had been waiting for it to happen. His first reactions were like those of many young men at the time, who saw this as a romantic and heroic conflict. He was also in debt by this stage, having lived beyond his means and without earning an income, and the war provided a way out of financial trouble.

Sassoon joined the Sussex **Yeomanry** almost immediately as a cavalry officer. He does not seem to have had any doubts

Siegfried Sassoon outside the family home of Weirleigh, looking very much the fox-hunting country gentleman.

about the decision (unlike men such as Rosenberg, who were full of misgivings about their lack of **patriotic** feelings). However, following a riding injury in which he broke his arm, and owing to the fact that he was becoming increasingly bored, in May 1915 he transferred to the Royal Welch Fusiliers. He went into the ranks as an officer (a second lieutenant).

Meeting Robert Graves
The Royal Welch Fusiliers was also the **regiment** of another poet, Robert Graves (see pages 43–46), whom Sassoon met for the first time shortly after his arrival in France in November 1915. Graves speaks about their meeting in the **company mess** in his book, *Goodbye to All That*:

'I noticed *The Essays of Lionel Johnson* lying on the table. It was the first book I had seen in France (except my own Keats and Blake) that was neither a military textbook or a rubbishy novel. I stole a look at the fly-leaf, and the name [of the owner] was Siegfried Sassoon.'

Graves goes on to talk about an interesting exchange between the two young poets over war and verse:

'We went to the cake shop and ate cream buns. At this time I was getting my first book of poems, *Over the Brazier*, ready for the press; I had one or two drafts in my pocket-book and showed them to Siegfried. He frowned and said that war should not be written about in such a realistic way… Siegfried had not yet been in the **trenches**. I told him, in my old-soldier manner, that he would soon change his style.'

Graves, of course, was completely right. Sassoon's feelings about the war were to change radically over the next few years. Bitter experience of fighting and the loss of good friends inevitably took its toll on his early idealism. He was to become one of the most direct and realistic writers on conditions in the trenches and the lives of ordinary soldiers.

Sassoon's poetry reflects the changes in his attitude. His early works celebrate the fighting and the just cause ('the self-glorifying feelings of a young man about to go to the front for the first time'). Later ones are bitter and satirical pieces blaming what he saw as the old men sitting safely in the cities, dragging the war out longer than it needed to go on.

'Mad Jack'

For a man who showed no signs of having any particular social conscience before the war broke out, Sassoon went on to develop a great interest and care for his men, something which comes through in his writing. He won the **Military Cross** the following year for bringing back a wounded soldier out of no-man's land whilst under heavy fire from the enemy. He constantly risked his life for others – for which reason he became known as 'Mad Jack' – developing a strong sense of responsibility towards the men under his command. This is one of Sassoon's hallmarks, along with his contempt for the people sitting comfortably in London, profiting from the war and doing very little to help end it. In this he included career politicians, bankers and businessmen, and women who only saw their soldiers as heroes, waving them gaily off to the front, oblivious to the horror into which they were sending them.

Craiglockhart

Sassoon was wounded in April 1917 and was sent back to Britain. In July of that year he was sent to the hospital of Craiglockhart, where he was to spend four months recovering. During that time he met Wilfred Owen (see pages 31–36). Sassoon's health improved to some degree, and his feelings developed from anger towards the incompetent generals and leaders to direct anti-war feelings. These found expression in a pamphlet he called *Soldier's Declaration*, in which he said: 'I am making this statement as an act of wilful defiance of military authority, because I believe that the war is being deliberately prolonged by those who have the power to end it.' This was one of the bravest acts that this brave man had ever done. He had been helped by well-known **pacifist** friends, notably Ottoline Morrell, John Middleton Murry and Bertrand Russell.

A photograph of Siegfried Sassoon in France in 1916.

Sassoon sent *Soldier's Declaration* to his commanding officer. He then circulated copies to friends and influential people, including newspaper editors – it appeared in *The Times*, *Manchester Guardian*, *Daily Telegraph* and *Bradford Pioneer*. As this was a time of war, he could have been **court marshalled** and sentenced to death. However, through the intervention of friends such as Robert Graves (who was convalescing on the Isle of Wight), Sassoon was put in front of a medical examination board. He was saved by being found too deeply affected by the trauma of war to be held responsible for his writing.

> "   "
>
> *Base Details* is one of Sassoon's later poems:
>
> 'If I were fierce, and bald, and short of breath,
> I'd live with scarlet Majors at the Base,
> And speed glum heroes up the line to death.
> You'd see me with my puffy petulant face,
> Guzzling and gulping in the best hotel,
> Reading the Roll of Honour. "Poor young chap,"
> I'd say – "I used to know his father well;
> Yes, we've lost heavily in this last scrap."
> And when the war is done and youth stone dead,
> I'd toddle safely home and die – in bed.'

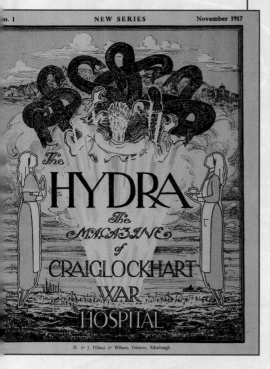

The *Hydra* was a literary magazine produced by the patients of Craighlockhart. Siegfried Sassoon contributed a poem called *Dreamers* to the 1 September 1917 edition.

Sassoon's reaction was to ask to be allowed to go back to the fighting with his men. At least he understood them and felt comfortable sharing the hard and precarious life of a soldier. Like Wilfred Owen, Sassoon could not justify sitting out the war safely in England. He went first to the Middle East to fight against Turkey and then finally back to France, where he was once again wounded. Unlike Owen, however, Sassoon survived the war.

Siegfried Sassoon officially left the army in March 1919. He spent the next few years cultivating the literary establishment, mostly in London. He met many famous writers, including Thomas Hardy, John Galsworthy and Walter de la Mare, and embarked on editing the as yet unpublished poetry of Wilfred Owen. He also became literary editor of the *Daily Herald* newspaper. There he helped to launch the writing career of his friend Edmund Blunden (see page 49), and to get the names of Charles Sorley (pages 17–21) and Isaac Rosenberg (pages 22–26) more widely known after their deaths.

However, his greatest works in the years after the First World War were his six volumes of fictionalized autobiography – *Memoirs of a Fox Hunting Man* (1928), *Memoirs of an Infantry Officer* (1930), *Sherston's Progress* (1936), *The Old Century and Seven More Years* (1938), *The Weald of Youth* (1942) and *Siegfried's Journey* (1945). He married Hester Gatty in 1933 and they had one son, George, born in 1936. However, the marriage ended in divorce in 1945. In 1953 he was made an honorary fellow of Clare College, Cambridge, where he had been an undergraduate, in recognition of his prose and poetry works. He died in 1967, in his early eighties.

Robert Graves

Robert Graves survived the battles of the Great War, despite being seriously wounded, and went on to live a long and creative life. He wrote a very famous account of his time during and just after the war called *Goodbye to All That*. Published in 1929, it contains not only his own thoughts, feelings and experiences of the times, but also brilliant sketches of other poets he came to know during the conflict, including Wilfred Owen (see pages 31–36), Siegfried Sassoon (pages 37–42) and Edmund Blunden (page 49).

London and school

Robert Ranke Graves was born in London in 1895. His father Alfred Perceval Graves, originally from Dublin, was an inspector of schools in Southwark. He had collected Irish songs and ballads and had composed a popular song, *Father O'Flynn*. His son Robert was brought up in a large and chaotic family, with Irish, Scottish and German roots.

The schoolboy, Robert Graves, at Charterhouse School. He was later to write scathingly about his time there.

They were from the upper middle classes, and had servants to cook for them and look after the children. His early schooling was haphazard – he attended a series of different schools.

Eventually, when he was twelve years old, Graves went to the well-known **public school**, Charterhouse. He disliked the place enormously, but it formed a large part of his life at the time. Graves boarded there, which meant that he saw little of his parents. He found it hard to fit in and was bullied, until at the suggestion of another boy, he took up boxing. Graves proved good at the sport, though he had his nose broken.

'I had just finished with Charterhouse and gone up to Harlech [where the Graves family often took holidays], when England declared war on Germany. A day or two later I decided to enlist. In the first place, though the papers predicted only a very short war – over by Christmas at the outside – I hoped that it might last long enough to delay my going to Oxford, which I dreaded… In the second place, I was outraged to read of the Germans' cynical violation of Belgian neutrality.'
From *Goodbye to All That*, 1929

This was not corrected until his time in the army. During the war the Germans used poison gas as a weapon. The British authorities brought out a special gas mask for the troops but Graves could not breathe through his nose, so it was of no use to him. Although an army surgeon operated on him to correct the problem, he did not do a very good job. Graves could only breathe through one nostril for the rest of his life.

Surviving the trenches

Soon after the outbreak of war, Graves enlisted in the Royal Welch Fusiliers, the **regiment** that Siegfried Sassoon was to join the following year. Graves wrote in *Goodbye to All That*:

'In the **trenches**, a few months later, I happened to belong to a **company mess** in which four of us young officers out of five had… either German mothers or neutralised German fathers. One of them said: "I'm glad I joined when I did. If I'd put it off for a month or two, they'd have accused me of being a German spy."'

Robert Graves survived the war and went on to have a long and successful literary career. He died in 1985, at the age of 90.

Graves was to see a lot of action in the trenches over the next two or three years. He was, however, a survivor. Many of his friends were killed. On several occasions the **platoon** he was in were poised, ready to go over the top to almost certain death, when the command to withdraw from the attack came through, thus saving his life. Luck and his determination to survive saved him.

Others were not so lucky. Talking about the disastrous Battle of Loos in 1915, Graves notes:

'Gradually the noise died down, and at last a message came from the brigade that we would not be needed. It had been another dud show, chiefly notorious for the death of Charles Sorley, a twenty-year-old captain in the Suffolks, one of the three poets of importance killed during the war [the other two were Isaac Rosenberg and Wilfred Owen]... So ended the operations for 1915.'

During the war, Graves brought out two volumes of poetry – *Over the Brazier* (1916) and *Fairies and Fusiliers* (1917). These contained 46 poems of the war years, including ones about the trenches, such as *The Assault Heroic*, *A Dead Boche*, *1915* and *The Next War*.

The actor, Derek Jacobi, in the role of the Roman, Claudius, in the BBC dramatization of Graves's novel, *I Claudius*.

A return to peacetime writing

After the war, Graves became a writer of some importance, but was known mainly for his novels. He was to write *I Claudius* (1934), *Claudius the God* (1934) and *Count Belisarius* (1938). These works of prose fiction brought him money and some fame. He taught for a while after the war in Egypt, as Professor of English Literature at the new Royal Egyptian University in

The beautiful mountain village of Deja on the Spanish Island of Majorca. Robert Graves lived here for many years and is buried in the small churchyard overlooking the sea.

Cairo, then moved to the Spanish island of Majorca, where he spent much of the rest of his very long life. In 1961 he became a professor of poetry at Oxford University, a post he held until 1966. Graves died in 1985, in his 90th year, and is buried in the small town of Deja on the rocky north coast of Majorca.

> 'Near Martinpuich that night of hell
> Two men were struck by the same shell,
> Together tumbling in one heap
> Senseless and limp like slaughtered sheep.
>
> One was a pale eighteen-year-old,
> Blue-eyed and thin and not too bold...
>
> The other came from far-off lands
> With bristling chin and whiskered hands,...
>
> Yet in death this cut-throat wild
> Groaned 'Mother! Mother! Like a child,
> While that poor innocent in man's clothes
> Died cursing God with brutal oaths.'
>
> From Graves's poem The Leveller, 1916

Ivor Gurney

Ivor Gurney was from a humble Gloucestershire background. He was very interested in music and this influenced his poetry, which was unconventional and original in character. Although Gurney survived the war, he was put in a mental asylum in 1922. As one commentator has said of him:

'I believe that what we have is the ruins of a major poet, and that his madness is of the essence of the fragments of really original poetry he left.'

A musical beginning

Gurney was born in Gloucester on 28 August 1890. He went to the King's School in that town, and was a choirboy there. His interest in music was strong from a very early age, and pre-dated his poetry. After school he won a **scholarship** to the Royal College of Music.

War

Gurney applied to join the Gloucester **Regiment** at the beginning of the war. He was initially turned down due to his very poor eyesight. However, once it had become obvious to the authorities that more men were needed and that the war was going to last longer than originally thought, Gurney was accepted in 1915. He was sent to the Western Front in France and was quickly involved with the fighting there. He was wounded in April 1917 (the same year in which his collection of war poems, called *Severn and Somme*, appeared) but was back in action on the front by the summer. At the Battle of Passchendaele – a major offensive that gained very little, but cost hundreds of thousands of lives – Gurney was gassed. Once again he was removed from the **trenches**.

Ivor Gurney in the uniform of the Gloucester Regiment, which he joined in 1915.

Gurney survived the gas attack but his mind was unhinged. He was discharged from the army in 1918, just before the war officially ended. In 1922 he was committed to an asylum, from where he used to write to friends asking them to rescue him. His medical record describes his illness at the time as 'manic/depressive psychosis, aggravated but not caused by the war'.

Gurney's poetry about the war contains great anger at the waste of life and the insupportable misery and suffering the soldiers were being asked to cope with. In *The Silent One*, written in 1917, he talks about a dead soldier hanging from the barbed wire after one useless attack:

'Who for his hours of life had chattered through
Infinite lovely chatter of Bucks accent.'

The language Gurney uses is always starkly original and arresting. But although he survived the fighting physically, the war damaged his ability to create great verse. As we have seen, the medical authorities claimed that his mental illness pre-dated the war. The truth of the matter, however, will never be known. He eventually died on 26 December 1937, at an asylum in Dartford, Kent.

> "
> Gas was one of the things soldier most feared about an enemy attack. Wilfred Owen's great and terrible poem *Dulce Et Decorum Est* describes the effects of wartime gas attacks on a human being:
>
> '*Gas! GAS! Quick, boys! – An ecstasy of fumbling,*
> *Fitting the clumsy helmets just in time;*
> *But someone still was yelling out and stumbling*
> *And floundering like a man in fire or lime –*
> *Dim, through the misty panes and thick green light*
> *As under a green sea, I saw him drowning…*
>
> *And watch the white eyes writhing in his face*
> *… the blood*
> *Come gargling from the froth-corrupted lungs…*'
> "

Other men's flowers

These are some of the other poets who wrote during the war.

Richard Aldington (1892–1962)

Richard Aldington was born in Hampshire and went to London University. He joined the army and served in France until 1918. He suffered a bad gas attack but survived the fighting. Aldington wrote poetry and novels, many of which are to do with his experiences in the war. *Death of a Hero* is a novel about a young officer and *Images of War* (published in 1919) is a collection of his poems from this period.

Edmund Blunden (1896–1974)

Edmund Blunden was born in London in 1896 and later lived in Kent. He went to Christ's Hospital School and then on to Queen's College at Oxford University. He was destined for an academic and literary life, but the war interrupted that. He joined the Royal Sussex **Regiment**, fighting at the Battles of Ypres and the Somme. He won the **Military Cross** for bravery in combat. Blunden survived the war and resumed his academic career, teaching in Tokyo, Hong Kong and at Oxford. He wrote biographies of many famous literary men and published several volumes of verse. Poems relating to his experiences in the war include *Vlamertinghe: Passing the Chateau* and *Preparations for Victory*. He also wrote an important prose work, *Undertones of War* (1928).

Wilfrid Gibson (1878–1962)

Wilfrid Gibson was one of the oldest poets to serve in the First World War. At the time of joining the army he was in his late thirties, married, and had a family. His instincts were to support the poor and underprivileged in society. Before the war, Gibson had worked as a social worker in the East End of London. During the war, his poems reflect the views of the ordinary **private soldier**. For example, these lines are from *Breakfast* (1914):

'We ate our breakfast lying on our backs
Because the shells were screeching overhead.
I bet a rasher to a loaf of bread
That Hull United would beat Halifax.'

Julian Grenfell in the uniform of the Royal Dragoons. Grenfell was a professional soldier before the war broke out, and welcomed combat.

Julian Grenfell (1888–1915)

Julian Grenfell was the son of Lord Desborough and was educated at Eton School and Balliol College, Oxford. Julian Grenfell became known as the 'happy warrior'. He actively liked the idea of fighting. He saw it as a natural thing for men to do. Sensing his need for combat and adventure early on, he joined the Royal Dragoons in 1910, serving in India and South Africa. When war came, he saw it as the opportunity to release his desire for battle. However, he was inspired by personal motives, not a great **patriotic** urge to serve his country.

He wrote in a letter, 'One loves one's fellow-man so much more when one is bent on killing him.' It is hard for most people to understand what he meant by this. He also wrote one of the most popular poems of the war, *Into Battle*, published in *The Times* only a few days after Grenfell was killed in May 1915. It was interpreted as a patriotic poem (hence its popularity in the first place), but Grenfell and his poems are more complex than this simple emotion implies.

Herbert Read (1893–1968)

Herbert Read was born in Yorkshire and educated at Leeds University. Like Edmund Blunden, he survived the war and went on to have a career as a writer and academic. He served in the Yorkshire Regiment and was awarded the Military Cross. Two collections of his verse relate to his experiences in the **trenches**, *Songs of Chaos* (published in 1915) and *Naked Warriors* (published in 1919). Read also wrote prose autobiographical pieces on his life in the Great War, *In Retreat* (1925) and *Ambush* (1930). He worked in the Victoria and Albert Museum after the war and also as Professor of Fine Art at Edinburgh University.

Edward Thomas (1878–1917)

Edward Thomas was from a Welsh family, but was born in London in March 1878. He attended St Paul's School and then went on to Lincoln College, Oxford, to study History. Thomas was struggling to become a writer when war broke out. Unlike most of the famous war poets, he was married with a wife, Helen, and a daughter, Myfanwy. He joined the army in 1915 and became a lieutenant in the Royal Artillery. Thomas was killed by a shell on 9 April 1917 near Arras. He wrote many fine war poems, including *In Memoriam* and *This is No Case of Petty Right or Wrong*, with the opening lines:

'This is no case of petty right or wrong
That politicians or philosophers
can judge. I hate not Germans, or grow hot
With love of Englishmen, to please the newspapers.'

John McCrae (1872–1918)

John McCrae was a Canadian by birth, educated at McGill University, and trained as a physician. He fought on the Western Front in 1914 with the Canadian Expeditionary Force, before being put in the Medical Corps. He died of pneumonia in 1918, while in charge of the Allied hospital in Boulogne in France. McCrae is remembered today as the author of probably the best-known of all poems of this period, *In Flanders Fields* (see below). It was written after he had taken part in the second Battle of Ypres.

> "   "
> 'In Flanders fields the poppies blow,
> Between the crosses, row on row
> That mark our place;
> …
> 'If ye break faith with us who die
> We shall not sleep, though poppies grow
> In Flanders fields.'
> The opening and closing lines of John McCrae's *In Flanders Fields*,
> which started the association of poppies with the war

Distant views

Many other poets also wrote about the First World War at the time. Some were from an older generation of men, too old to fight, who had been moulded in the Victorian era and often held very **patriotic** views. Some had sons or relatives fighting at the front; some were professionally involved in the war in one capacity or another. They all had views on the events, and they make interesting comparisons with those men fighting and writing from the frontline.

Rudyard Kipling

Rudyard Kipling was born in Bombay in 1865. He will be forever associated with the **British Empire** in India. He is best known for his novels set in India, *The Jungle Book* and *Kim*. He was a journalist who wrote many poems and articles about life in British-ruled India. However, he also wrote with great perception about army life and combat situations, because the British army in the 19th century was always involved in campaigns, including in India and Africa. For example, he went to South Africa at the outbreak of the Boer War in 1889, and produced a newspaper for the British troops.

During the First World War Kipling made a tour of the army camps in Britain and also visited the Western Front. Out of this came two pieces of prose writing, *The New Army* and *France at War*, in which he wrote with strong

A photograph of Rudyard Kipling, taken in 1910, when the author was in his mid-forties.

> " 'He led the **platoon** in a mile of open ground in the face of shell and machine-gun and was dropped at the further limit of the advance, after having emptied his pistol into a house full of Germans… He was senior **ensign** though only 18 years and 6 weeks. It was a short life. I'm sorry that the year's work ended in that one afternoon but – lots of people are in our position – and it is something to have bred such a man.' "
>
> From a letter by Kipling to L. C. Dunsterville on the death of his son John Kipling, 1915

anti-German feeling, calling Germany 'the beast'. Kipling also wrote a pamphlet on the Royal Navy, called *The Fringes of the Fleet*. In this he stated that had Britain used the Royal Navy to greater effect in the early stages of the war (it was the largest in the world at the time), then the fighting would not have gone on for so long.

In several of his poems, Kipling wrote with feeling about the situation of the ordinary soldiers and the lies that were fed to them by politicians and senior officers. His only son, John, was killed within weeks of arriving in France, at the Battle of Loos. In a poem written in 1918, called *Common Form*, he says:

'If any question why we died
Tell them, because our fathers lied.'

Six years after the war ended, he wrote another bitter poem, called *A Dead Statesman*. Rudyard Kipling died in 1936.

Thomas Hardy

Like Kipling, Thomas Hardy wrote with some insight and complexity about the war, which had started when he was was already 74 years old. Born in 1840, only three years after the young Queen Victoria had come to the throne, Hardy became one of the greatest novelists and poets writing in the English language. In *Channel Firing*, a poem written in 1914, Hardy portrayed the conflict that had just started as mindless. It was, he believed, an admission of failure on the parts of the powerful people in society, who should have been able to prevent it from occurring. *And There was a Great Calm (On the signing of the* **Armistice**, *Nov. 11, 1918)* explores the pity and waste of war.

Hardy was from a different era to those men who were actively fighting. His values were more traditional. But nonetheless, he showed that a person could react with anger towards injustice and incompetence whilst at the same time remaining fundamentally patriotic.

Other men

There were other older men writing poetry at this time. G. K. Chesterton (1874–1936) and Sir Henry Newbolt (1862–1938) were leading writers of their day. They were employed by the **War Propaganda Bureau** to help mould public opinion in favour of the war and to strengthen the will to defeat Germany. One of the best-known of the '**propagandist**' poems is Newbolt's *The Schoolfellow*.

The great British novelist, Thomas Hardy, photographed outside his house in the 1920s. He was appalled by the waste of young life during the war.

> "
> *'Our game was his but yesteryear,*
> *We wished him back; we could not know*
> *The self-same hour we wished him here*
> *He led the line that broke the foe.*
>
> *Blood-red behind our guarded posts*
> *Sank as old and dying day;*
> *The battle ceased; the mingled hosts*
> *Weary and cheery went their way.'*
> "
> The first two verses of Newbolt's *The Schoolfellow*, 1914

Lasting impressions

Most people are familiar with the official memorials to the First World War. These include the Cenotaph in London, the minute's silence every year on **Armistice** Day (11 November), and the memorials in villages and towns across the length and breadth of the country. They are tributes to men who went to fight and never came back. There is even a grand memorial in Westminster Abbey to the war poets themselves. And of course there are more poems, mostly by lesser poets or by older men, or those who had not yet experienced life on the Western Front. Many of these poets spoke about the glory, **patriotism** and heroics of the war, and their works are probably more often read or quoted than any other of the poems. For example, Laurence Binyon's poem *For the Fallen* adorns many memorials and is very well known:

'They shall not grow old, as we that are left grow old:
Age shall not weary them, nor the years condemn.
At the going down of the sun and in the morning
We will remember them.'

In addition, works of autobiography such as Robert Grave's *Goodbye to All That*, Vera Brittain's *Testament of Youth*, and the various books by Siegfried Sassoon, such as *Memoirs of an Infantry Officer*, are still bought and read on a regular basis. They have achieved the status of classics. Indeed, Vera Brittain's personal history of the times was made into a highly successful history drama series for television.

However, the verse and other works of the great war poets have also endured the test of time. These poems are read in their own right for the acute feelings and direct experiences they convey to the reader. No history book could ever bring back the horrors of the war or invoke so many mixed and powerful feelings as these poems do. Great poems of war will always be read to remind us in vivid terms of what war is really like. And these poems were written by people who were well aware, certainly as time dragged on, of the absurdity and tragic waste of it all.

Timeline

1865	Birth of Rudyard Kipling.
1869	Birth of Laurence Binyon.
1872	Birth of John McCrae.
1878	Birth of Wilfrid Gibson.
1886	Birth of Siegfried Sassoon.
1887	Birth of Rupert Brooke.
1888	Birth of Julian Grenfell.
1890	Birth of Isaac Rosenberg. Birth of Ivor Gurney.
1893	Birth of Vera Brittain. Birth of Wilfred Owen.
1895	Birth of Charles Sorley. Birth of Robert Graves.
1896	Birth of Edmund Blunden.
1901	Death of Queen Victoria, Edward VII comes to the throne.
1908	H. H. Asquith becomes Prime Minister.
1910	Death of Edward VII, George V comes to the throne.
1914	Publication of Kipling's *The New Army in Training*. (August) Outbreak of war between Britain and Germany. (26 August) Opening of the Battle of Tannenberg. (5 September) Opening of the First Battle of the Marne. (14 September) Opening of the First Battle of the Aisne. (November) The opposing armies dig in, and trenches, barbed wire and machine guns become the norm for the fighting on the Western Front. (21 December) First German zeppelin air raid on Britain.
1915	Publication of Kipling's *France at War*. (19 February) British and French begin naval action against the Dardenelles, in Turkey. (22 April) Second Battle of Ypres begins. (February) British, Australian and New Zealand troops land on Gallipoli Peninsula in Turkey. (23 April) Death of Rupert Brooke. (April) Death of Julian Grenfell. (2 May) Opening of great Austro-German offensive against Russia in Galicia. (7 May) Sinking of the passenger liner *Lusitania* by a German U-boat off the Irish coast.

(9 May) Opening of the Second Battle of Artois on the Western Front.

(23 May) Italy declares war on Austria-Hungary.

(22 September) Opening of Second Battle of Champagne on the Western Front.

(3–5 October) Anglo-French force lands at Salonika, Greece.

(13 October) Death of Charles Sorley.

(15 December) Field Marshal Douglas Haig becomes Commander-in-Chief of the **British Expeditionary Force**.

1916 Publication of *Soldier Poets: Songs of the Fighting Men*, a collection of 72 poems, mostly idealistic and romanticized views on the war.

Publication of Graves's *Over the Brazier*.

(21 February) Beginning of ten-month Battle of Verdun in France.

(24 April) Beginning of the Easter Rising revolt against British rule in Ireland on Easter Monday.

(27 April) Field Marshal Lord Kitchener, British Secretary of State for War, asks for American military assistance.

(1 July) Opening of the Battle of the Somme. British Army suffers nearly 60,000 casualties on the first day.

(15 September) First use of tanks by the British, on the Somme battlefield.

(28 November) First German airplane raid on London.

(5 December) Asquith resigns as Prime Minister. He is replaced by David Lloyd George.

1917 Publication of Sassoon's *The Old Huntsman*.

Publication of Graves's *Fairies and Fusiliers*.

(9 January) German leaders decide to launch unrestricted U-boat warfare.

(3 February) USA severs relations with Germany.

(6 April) USA declares war on Germany.

(26 June) First US troops (1st Division) arrive in France.

(31 July) Passchendaele offensive (Third Battle of Ypres) opens in Flanders.

(20 November) British launch surprise tank attack at Cambrai in France.

1918 Publication of Sassoon's *Counter-Attack*.

(January) Death of John McCrae.

(21 March) Germans launch first of their great 1918 assaults against British Army (Battle of Picardy).

(1 April) Death of Isaac Rosenberg.

1918	(9 April) Germans launch second assault of their 1918 offensive (Battle of the Lys).
	(27 May) Opening of third phase of 1918 German offensive (Third Battle of the Aisne).
	(9 June) Opening of fourth phase of 1918 German offensive (Battle of the Matz).
	(15 July) Opening of last phase of German offensive (Second Battle of the Marne).
	(18 July) Allied counterattack seizes strategical initiative from Germans; nine US divisions participate.
	(8 August) Opening of Battle of Amiens.
	(3–4 October) Germans and Austrians send notes to US President Woodrow Wilson requesting an **armistice**.
	(4 November) Death of Wilfred Owen.
	(11 November) Armistice goes into effect at 11 a.m., the eleventh day of the eleventh month.
1919	(18 January) Peace negotiations start at Paris.
	(25 January) Peace conference accepts principle of League of Nations.
	(28 June) Treaty of Versailles signed in the Hall of Mirrors at Versailles.
1920	Publication of Edward Thomas's *Collected Poems*.
	Publication of Wilfred Owen's *Collected Poems* (put together by Siegfried Sassoon).
1926	Publication of Sassoon's *Satirical Poems*.
	Publication of Wilfred Gibson's *Collected Poems 1905–1925*.
1928	Publication of Sassoon's *The Heart's Journey*.
	Publication of Sassoon's *Memoirs of a Fox-Hunting Man*.
1930	Publication of Sassoon's *Memoirs of an Infantry Officer*.
1936	Death of Rudyard Kipling.
1937	Publication of Rosenberg's *Collected Works*.
	Death of Ivor Gurney.
1943	Death of Laurence Binyon.
1962	Death of Wilfrid Gibson.
1967	Death of Siegfried Sassoon.
1970	Death of Vera Brittain.
1974	Death of Edmund Blunden.
1985	Death of Robert Graves.

Glossary

anthology collection of works (short stories or poems) from one or several writers

anti-semitic prejudiced against jews

armistice truce or suspension of fighting. The term Armistice refers to 11 November 1918, when hostilities in the First World War ceased.

Austro-Hungarian Empire area ruled over by the Royal House of Austria (the Hapsburgs), including large parts of Hungary. The Empire split up after the First World War, when Austria and Hungary both declared themselves republics (countries with an elected government or president rather than a king or queen).

Balkans the area of south-east Europe that includes Albania, Bosnia, Yugoslavia, Bulgaria, Croatia, Greece, Romania, Slovenia and part of Turkey

battalion body of men in the army made up of four or five companies (about 120 men each) and commanded by a lieutenant colonel

blithely casually, in a care-free manner

British Empire countries ruled over by Britain between the 17th and 20th centuries. In the years before the outbreak of the First World War, the British Empire was at its height and was the largest empire the world had known.

British Expeditionary Force part of the British Army. At the outbreak of the First World War it was sent to France to fight alongside the French and Belgian armies, to halt the advance of the Germans. It eventually numbered over a million men.

cadet corps groups of boys and young men at public schools around Britain who were given military training. These were very popular during the First World War.

civilian person who does not serve in the armed forces

company mess place where soldiers eat together. A company is a unit in the British Army.

court marshalled tried in front of a military court (rather than a civil court) for breaking military laws. In wartime, the penalty for crimes such as cowardice or desertion was death by firing squad.

ensign lowest ranking officer in the British Army

enterprising someone who is ready to take advantage of a situation, and who takes the initiative

epitome perfect example of something

establishment those in society who hold political and economic power

governess woman employed by a well-to-do family to look after and educate a child or children at home

graduate when a person has passed their exams at university and receives their degree

homosexuality being physically and emotionally attracted to people of the same sex

housemaster teacher in charge of a 'house' at a public school. Pupils were divided up into 'houses', or buildings, where they lived during term time. The houses would compete in games, for example.

hypocrisy saying one thing but believing another

incongruous something that does not fit or is unsuitable

matriculation university examination that had to be passed in order to enter a university

Military Cross medal awarded to officers for bravery. It was introduced during the First World War.

pacifism belief that war is not justified under any circumstances, and that differences between countries should always be worked out by discussion, not killing

patriotism unquestioning love and support for one's own country

patron person who takes a special interest in someone else, especially a struggling artist or writer. A patron offers them financial help and introductions to important and influential people.

platoon one of the smallest divisions in the army

populist someone who understands and appeals to the mass of people

posthumous occuring after the death of someone

preparatory school a private school for primary age pupils that prepares them for their next school

private soldier lowest ranking soldier in the army

proffered given

propaganda term (usually used negatively) to describe writing or speech that is used to manipulate a situation in favour of the opinions and ideas of the person writing or speaking

public school a traditional private school for the privileged members of British society. Famous schools include Eton, Rugby, Harrow, Winchester and Charterhouse.

purged emptied or cleaned

puritan keeping to a strict moral code, which includes denying oneself pleasurable things

regiment unit of soldiers in the armed forces. Their commander is called a colonel.

religious persecution harassment of people on grounds of their religion

Romantic term describing a movement amongst poets and artists of the late 18th century. Romantic poets, such as Blake and Shelley, emphasized the supremacy of the individual, of childhood, of the imagination and of nature over such things as society, adulthood, reason and urbanization. Since the Romantic period, the term has been applied to those who have sympathy with the Romantic view.

satirical term describing a style of writing that ridicules (laughs at) something that is seen to be false, hypocritical or stupid

scholarship grant or sum of money that a student gets after passing exams. The money is used to support them while at school or university.

sentimental usually a negative term, used to describe someone who shows excessive emotion

sentry soldier who is on guard

shell-shock mental illness caused by severe stress, especially among soldiers at war

shrapnel deadly fragments of metal thrown out by the explosion of a special shell fired from a cannon. The weapon was invented by a General Shrapnel in the early 19th century.

sloth laziness

socialist person who believes that the community should own, run and organize economic and political institutions in society, rather than private individuals or businesses

stalemate term used to describe a situation in a conflict in which neither side can get the upper hand to take victory

steeple-chase type of horse race that takes place across country and includes some obstacles to jump over

sub-lieutenant rank in the army or navy

superlative of the greatest kind, most extreme

symmetry balance or equal weight on both sides of a line

technical school school developed to train pupils in useful trades, more closely allied with business and work than the Public schools with their emphasis on classical studies

temperance society movement that grew in 19th-century America and Great Britain to combat the increasing drunkenness that was thought to be threatening social order

trenches ditches dug into the earth to give troops shelter from enemy fire

Voluntary Aid Detachment (VAD) unit set up during the First World War for untrained women to help in hospitals in Britain, Europe and the Middle East. Trained and professional nurses often looked down on VAD nurses.

War Propaganda Bureau (WPB) part of the War Office, used to put across important messages from the Government to the public. It employed several well-known literary men to add weight to its messages.

Yeomanry a cavalry force in the British Army

Places of interest, websites and further reading

Places of interest

The Cenotaph, London – the Cenotaph is located in London's Whitehall and is a memorial to all those who died during the two world wars. A remembrance service is held each year at 11 a.m. on the Sunday nearest to 11 November, the date the Armistice was signed.

Imperial War Museum, London – the Imperial War Museum in London covers all aspects of life in wartime, both at the frontline and back at home. Many of the collections include material relevant to the First World War, and it is even possible to see original manuscripts written by many of the war poets.

Memorial to the War Poets, Westminster Abbey, London – this memorial to sixteen First World War poets is located in the Poet's Corner of Westminster Abbey.

National Army Museum, Chelsea, London – the museum of the British Army, which tells the story of the British Army from the Battle of Agincourt in the 15th century to the present day.

Websites

http://www.iwm.org.uk/
The website of the Imperial War Museum in London. In addition to information about the museum itself, the website is also home to numerous online exhibitions, including several on the First World War.

http://www.spartacus.schoolnet.co.uk/
The *Spartacus* website includes a useful online encyclopedia of the First World War.

http://www.robertgraves.org/
The website of the St John's College Robert Graves Trust. It contains lots of information about Graves' life and work, and there are also lots of links to other useful websites on war poets.

Further reading

Goodbye to All That, Robert Graves (Penguin, 1999)

Men Who March Away, edited by I. M. Parsons (Chatto and Windus, 1965)

Out of Battle: The Poetry of the Great War, Jon Silkin (Routledge, 1972)

The Penguin Book of First World War Poetry, edited by Jon Silkin (Penguin, 1979)

Poetry of the Great War, edited by Dominic Hibberd and John Onions (Palgrave Macmillan, 1986)

The Regeneration Trilogy, Pat Barker (Penguin, 1992)

Scars Upon My Heart; Women's Poetry and Verse of the First World War, edited by Catherine Reilly (Virago, 1981)

Up the Line to Death: The War Poets 1914–1918 (Methuen, 1964)

Index